Amazing Inventions

Inventing Refrigerators

by Rebecca Donnelly

www.focusreaders.com

Focus Readers is distributed by North Star Editions:
sales@northstareditions.com | 888-417-0195

Produced for Focus Readers by Red Line Editorial.

Photographs ©: Shutterstock Images, cover, 1, 4, 6, 12, 14–15, 16, 19, 21, 22, 27, 29; Detroit Publishing Co./Library of Congress, 8; Photo 12/Universal Images Group/Getty Images, 11; Karl Sandels/Historisk Bildbyrå/Mustang media/Heritage Images/Heritage Image Partnership Ltd/Alamy, 25

Library of Congress Cataloging-in-Publication Data
Library of Congress Cataloging-in-Publication Data is available on the Library of Congress website.

ISBN
978-1-63739-048-1 (hardcover)
978-1-63739-102-0 (paperback)
978-1-63739-207-2 (ebook pdf)
978-1-63739-156-3 (hosted ebook)

Printed in the United States of America
Mankato, MN
012022

About the Author

Rebecca Donnelly is a librarian and writer. She loves to read and write about science and history. Rebecca lives in northern New York State.

Table of Contents

Chapter 1

Keeping Food Cool

A girl and her dad get home from the store. They bought fresh groceries for the week. They put this food in their refrigerator. The girl sets milk on a shelf. Vegetables go in a drawer.

 In many fridges, a drawer called a crisper helps keep fruits and vegetables fresh longer.

 On some fridges, a dispenser on the door can release ice or water.

The girl's dad takes chicken out of the fridge. He placed it there earlier to **thaw**. Now, he cooks it for dinner. The girl gets their drinks.

She pours water and ice from the fridge's **dispenser**.

Then it's time to eat. For dessert, they both have ice cream from the freezer. After the meal, they put the leftovers in the fridge. They will eat this food tomorrow. The refrigerator will keep it safe and cool.

Did You Know?

People can reduce food waste by eating what's in their fridge before buying more food.

Chapter 2

Refrigeration History

Long ago, people learned that food lasts longer when it stays cool. For many years, people used ice to cool food. They cut ice from frozen lakes and rivers. They kept this ice in buildings or under the ground.

 People stored large blocks of ice in buildings called icehouses.

People stored their food in these places as well. The ice kept it cool.

In 1802, a farmer invented the icebox. This **insulated** box had several shelves inside. One shelf held a block of ice. Other shelves were for food. People could keep food cool inside their homes.

Early refrigerators were invented in the 1800s. Instead of ice, these fridges used **coolant**. A **compressor** sent the coolant through long tubes. The coolant took heat away

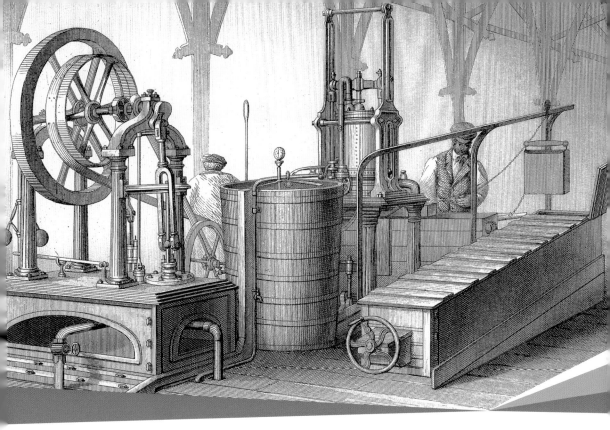

 Early refrigeration machines didn't use electricity. They used mechanical power instead.

from the area where the food sat.

This kept the food cold.

The first electric fridges were made in the 1910s. However, few people had them in their homes.

 By 1950, more than 80 percent of homes in the United States had a fridge.

These fridges cost a lot. Some used dangerous gases as coolant. And many didn't work very well. By the 1930s, fridges cost less and worked better. Many families began buying them.

Inventors continued improving refrigerators. They added new features. Freezer sections are one example. Later on, ice makers and water dispensers became common. By the 2000s, some fridges could even connect to the internet.

Did You Know?

The Monitor Top refrigerator came out in 1927. It was the first fridge that many families bought.

Smart Refrigerators

A smart refrigerator has a **computer chip** inside. It uses the internet to send and receive information. For example, a **sensor** may tell if the fridge door didn't close. It can send a message to a person's phone. Or a camera may show what's in the fridge. People can see what's inside, so they know what food they need to buy. A smart fridge often has a display screen on the door. The screen shows the settings. It may also let people go online. They can use it to check websites or play games.

People can use a smartphone to control a smart fridge.

Chapter 3

How a Fridge Works

A refrigerator stays cool by taking heat away from the food compartment. Coolant moves through small pipes in the refrigerator. The coolant **absorbs** heat from inside the fridge.

 The pipes that carry coolant curve back and forth. A panel separates them from the food.

Then it carries that heat out of the refrigerator. This process is called the refrigeration cycle. It has four main steps.

First, liquid coolant flows to the evaporator. Here, a fan blows heat from the food compartment over curved pipes. Coolant is inside the pipes. As the pipes heat up, the coolant turns into gas.

This gas flows to the compressor. The compressor is a pump. In step two, this pump squeezes the

 A fridge's compressor warms the coolant by pressing on it.

gas. As a result, the gas becomes even warmer.

Third, the coolant flows through the condenser. This part is located on the back of the refrigerator.

The condenser looks like a long tube that curves back and forth. As coolant moves through the curves, it loses heat. The heat goes out into the air. And the coolant turns back into a liquid.

In step four, the liquid coolant flows to the expansion valve. This part slows the coolant's flow. Losing

Did You Know?

Air conditioners use the refrigeration cycle to cool buildings.

The Refrigeration Cycle

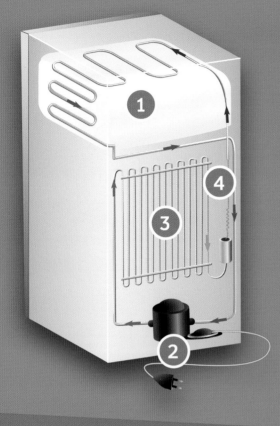

1. Cold liquid coolant flows through the evaporator. The coolant heats up and turns into a gas.

2. The compressor squeezes the coolant, which is still a gas.

3. The coolant releases heat and turns back into a liquid as it flows through the condenser.

4. The liquid coolant flows through the expansion valve and back into the evaporator.

speed cools the coolant even more. After this last step, coolant flows back to the evaporator. The cycle can begin again.

Chapter 4

The Impact of Fridges

Mold and **bacteria** can grow on food. These things can make people sick. However, they grow slowly in cool places. By keeping food cold, refrigerators help food stay safe to eat.

 Many foods go bad more quickly if they are not kept in a fridge.

Before refrigerators, people used ice to keep food cool. Workers carried ice to homes and businesses. But this ice could be hard to move. Ice blocks were thick and heavy. And if they melted, the food went bad.

Refrigerators made storing food much easier. They could work

Did You Know?

Most bacteria will not grow below 40 degrees Fahrenheit (4.4°C).

> **Wagons carried large blocks of ice. Some blocks weighed more than 75 pounds (34 kg).**

anywhere that had electricity. Food could last for days with no ice. Stores and restaurants could buy more food and keep it from going bad. So could families.

People began changing the way they shopped.

Refrigerators also changed the way food got to stores. Stores get food from farms and factories. But some of this food needs to stay cold. Otherwise, it will spoil. Refrigerators made it easy to keep

Did You Know?

Some medicines need to stay cool. Hospitals store them in refrigerators or freezers.

 Stores use large refrigerators to keep products cool before people buy them.

food cool on trucks, trains, and ships. That meant more people could buy foods from faraway places. Stores could also buy and keep more options for their customers. As a result, people had more choices of what to eat.

FOCUS ON
Inventing Refrigerators

Write your answers on a separate piece of paper.

1. Write a paragraph that describes the four steps of the refrigeration cycle.

2. If you were an inventor, what new feature would you add to a refrigerator? Why?

3. When were the first refrigerators invented?
    A. in the 1800s
    B. in the 1930s
    C. in the 2000s

4. How could owning refrigerators affect how families shopped?
    A. Families would have less space for food.
    B. Families could keep food longer, so they could buy more food at a time.
    C. Families couldn't keep food as long, so they had to buy less food at a time.

5. What does **groceries** mean in this book?

*They bought fresh **groceries** for the week. They put this food in their refrigerator.*

    A. toys bought from a store
    B. food bought from a store
    C. food taken from a garden

6. What does **leftovers** mean in this book?

*After the meal, they put the **leftovers** in the fridge. They will eat this food tomorrow.*

    A. plates and cups
    B. forks and knives
    C. extra food

Answer key on page 32.

Glossary

absorbs
Takes in.

bacteria
Tiny living things that can be either useful or harmful.

compressor
A machine used to pump, press, or squeeze.

computer chip
A small device that controls the actions of a computer or other machine.

coolant
Liquid or gas that flows through pipes or coils to make something cooler.

dispenser
A device that gives out small amounts of something.

insulated
Having a layer or coating that stops heat from getting in or out.

sensor
A device that collects and reports information.

thaw
To get warmer and unfreeze.

To Learn More

BOOKS

Bethea, Nikole Brooks. *Refrigerators*. Minneapolis: Jump!, 2021.

Rebman, Nick. *Earth-Friendly Eating*. Lake Elmo, MN: Focus Readers, 2022.

Spalding, Maddie. *Solids, Liquids, and Gases*. Mankato, MN: The Child's World, 2020.

NOTE TO EDUCATORS

Visit **www.focusreaders.com** to find lesson plans, activities, links, and other resources related to this title.

Index

B
bacteria, 23–24

C
compressor, 10, 18, 21
condenser, 19–21
coolant, 10, 12, 17–21

E
electricity, 11, 25
evaporator, 18, 21
expansion valve, 20–21

F
fan, 18
freezers, 7, 13, 26

I
ice, 7, 9–10, 13, 24–25
icebox, 10

P
pipes, 17–18

R
refrigeration cycle, 18–21
restaurants, 25

S
smart refrigerator, 14
stores, 5, 25–27

T
tubes, 10, 20

Answer Key: 1. Answers will vary; **2.** Answers will vary; **3.** A; **4.** B; **5.** B; **6.** C